Report to the Chairman, Subcommittee on Cybersecurity, Infrastructure Protection, and Security Technologies, House of Representatives, Committee on Homeland Security

July 2013

CRITICAL INFRASTRUCTURE PROTECTION

DHS Could Strengthen the Management of the Regional Resiliency Assessment Program

I0455427

July 2013

GAO Highlights

Highlights of GAO-13-616, a report to the Chairman, Subcommittee on Cybersecurity, Infrastructure Protection, and Security Technologies, Committee on Homeland Security, House of Representatives

CRITICAL INFRASTRUCTURE PROTECTION

DHS Could Strengthen the Management of the Regional Resiliency Assessment Program

Why GAO Did This Study

In October 2012, Hurricane Sandy caused widespread damage across multiple states. Further, threats to CI are not limited to natural disasters, as demonstrated by the terrorist attacks of September 11, 2001. In 2009, DHS initiated the RRAP, a voluntary program intended to assess regional resilience of CI. RRAP projects are to analyze a region's ability to adapt to changing conditions, and prepare for, withstand, and rapidly recover from disruptions.

GAO was asked to examine DHS's efforts to manage the program. GAO assessed the extent to which DHS (1) developed criteria for identifying RRAP project locations, (2) worked with states to conduct RRAP projects and share information with CI partners to promote resilience, and (3) is positioned to measure results associated with RRAP projects.

GAO reviewed applicable laws, DHS policies and procedures, and all 17 RRAP reports completed since the program inception in 2009. GAO also interviewed officials from 10 states with issued RRAP reports, DHS officials who conducted 20 RRAP projects from 2009 through 2012, and other federal officials representing nine departments and agencies involved in RRAP projects. While the results of the interviews are not generalizable, they provided insight.

What GAO Recommends

GAO recommends that DHS document final RRAP selections and develop a mechanism to measure whether RRAP participation influences facilities to make RRAP-related enhancements. DHS concurred with the recommendations.

View GAO-13-616. For more information, contact Stephen L. Caldwell at (202) 512-8777 or caldwells@gao.gov.

What GAO Found

The Department of Homeland Security (DHS) has developed nine criteria that consider various factors—including the willingness of various stakeholders, such as asset owners and operators, to participate and concentrations of high-risk critical infrastructure—when identifying possible locations for Regional Resiliency Assessment Program (RRAP) projects. According to DHS officials, final project selections are then made from a list of possible locations based on factors including geographic distribution and DHS priorities, among other considerations. However, it is unclear why some RRAP projects are recommended over others because DHS does not fully document why these decision are made. Federal internal control standards call for agencies to promptly record and clearly document transactions and significant events. Because DHS's selection process identifies a greater number of potential projects than DHS has the resources to perform, documenting why final selections are made would help ensure accountability, enabling DHS to provide evidence of its decision making.

DHS has worked with states to improve the process for conducting RRAP projects and is considering an approach for sharing resilience information with its critical infrastructure (CI) partners, including federal, state, local, and tribal officials. Since 2011, DHS has worked with states to improve the process for conducting RRAP projects, including more clearly defining the scope of projects. According to DHS officials, these efforts have been viewed favorably by states. DHS is currently considering an approach to more widely share resilience lessons learned with its CI partners, including a possible resiliency product or products that draw from completed RRAP projects. DHS officials stated that they engage CI partners in meetings and conferences where partners' resilience information needs are discussed and have been incorporating this input into their efforts to develop a resilience information sharing approach.

DHS has taken action to measure efforts to enhance security and resilience among facilities that participate in the RRAP, but faces challenges measuring results associated with RRAP projects. DHS performs security and vulnerability assessments at individual CI assets that participate in RRAPs projects as well as those that do not participate. Consistent with the *National Infrastructure Protection Plan*, DHS also performs periodic follow-ups among asset owners and operators that participate in these assessments with the intent of measuring their efforts to make enhancements arising out of these surveys and assessments. However, DHS does not measure how enhancements made at individual assets that participate in a RRAP project contribute to the overall results of the project. DHS officials stated that they face challenges measuring performance within and across RRAP projects because of the unique characteristics of each, including geographic diversity and differences among assets within projects. GAO recognizes that measuring performance within and among RRAP projects could be challenging, but DHS could better position itself to gain insights into projects' effects if it were to develop a mechanism to compare facilities that have participated in a RRAP project with those that have not, thus establishing building blocks for measuring its efforts to conduct RRAP projects. One approach could entail using DHS's assessment follow-up process to gather and analyze data to assess whether participation in a RRAP project influenced owners and operators to make related resilience enhancements.

_____ **United States Government Accountability Office**

Contents

Figures

Abbreviations

ANL	Argonne National Laboratory
CFATS	Chemical Facility Anti-Terrorism Standards
CI	critical infrastructure
CII	Critical Infrastructure Information
DHS	Department of Homeland Security
ECIP	Enhanced Critical Infrastructure Protection
FMFIA	Federal Managers' Financial Integrity Act of 1982
FOUO	For Official Use Only
HSPD	Homeland Security Presidential Directive
IP	Office of Infrastructure Protection
IST	Infrastructure Survey Tool
LENS	Link Encrypted Network System
NIPP	National Infrastructure Protection Plan
NISAC	National Infrastructure Simulation and Analysis Center
NPPD	National Protectorate Program Directorate
PCII	Protected Critical Infrastructure Information
PMP	project management plan
PSA	protective security advisor
PSCD	Protective Security Coordination Division
RRAP	Regional Resilience Assessment Program
SAV	site assistance visit
SLTTGCC	State, Local, Tribal and Territorial Government Coordinating Council
SSA	sector-specific agency
TVA	Tennessee Valley Authority

July 30, 2013

The Honorable Patrick Meehan
Chairman
Subcommittee on Cybersecurity, Infrastructure Protection
  and Security Technologies
Committee on Homeland Security
House of Representatives

Dear Mr. Chairman:

In the fall of 2012, the remnants of Hurricane Sandy caused widespread damage to infrastructure across multiple states and affected millions of people. Damage included flooding in the nation's financial center that affected major transportation systems and caused widespread and prolonged power outages. In March 2007, we reported that our nation's critical infrastructure (CI) continues to be vulnerable to a wide variety of threats.[1] Critical infrastructure is assets and systems, whether physical or virtual, so vital to the United States that their incapacity or destruction would have a negative or debilitating impact on national security, national economic security, national public health or safety, or any combination of those matters. Because the private sector owns the vast majority of the nation's critical infrastructure—banking and financial institutions, commercial facilities, and energy production and transmission facilities, among others—it is vital that the public and private sectors work together to protect these assets and systems. Furthermore, the extensive damage and long recovery required from natural disasters like Hurricane Sandy highlights the importance of critical infrastructure resilience. According to the Department of Homeland Security (DHS), resilience is the ability to adapt to changing conditions, and prepare for, withstand, and rapidly recover from disruptions.[2]

---

[1]GAO, *Critical Infrastructure: Challenges Remain in Protecting Key Sectors*, GAO-07-626T (Washington, D.C.: Mar. 20, 2007).

[2]DHS, Risk Steering Committee, *DHS Risk Lexicon* (Washington, D.C.; September 2010). DHS developed the risk lexicon to provide a common set of official terms and definitions to ease and improve the communication of risk-related issues for DHS and its partners.

In 2006, in accordance with section 201 of the Homeland Security Act of 2002, as amended, and other authorities and directives, DHS issued the *National Infrastructure Protection Plan* (NIPP),[3] which provides the overarching approach for integrating the nation's critical infrastructure protection and resilience activities into a single national effort.[4] The NIPP also outlines the roles and responsibilities of DHS with regard to CI protection and resilience and sector-specific agencies (SSA)—federal departments and agencies responsible for CI protection and resilience activities in each sector, such as the dams, energy, and transportation sectors. The NIPP emphasizes the importance of collaboration, partnering, and voluntary information sharing between DHS and private sector asset owners and operators, and state, local, and tribal governments. Among other things, the NIPP calls for DHS to analyze sector, cross-sector, and regional dependencies and interdependencies, to include cyber security, and share the results with CI partners, as appropriate. In addition, the NIPP calls for DHS to conduct and support comprehensive risk assessment programs for high-risk CI, identifying priorities across sectors and jurisdictions, and integrating CI protection and resilience programs with an all-hazards approach to domestic incident management.

Over the last several years, DHS has taken actions to develop or update programs to assess vulnerability and risk at CI facilities and within groups of related infrastructure, regions, and systems to place greater emphasis on resilience. One of these programs is the Regional Resiliency Assessment Program (RRAP), which was developed in 2009 by DHS's National Protectorate Program Directorate's (NPPD) Office of Infrastructure Protection (IP). The RRAP is an analysis of infrastructure clusters and systems in specific geographic areas or regions. Using the RRAP, DHS examines vulnerabilities, threats, and potential consequences to identify (1) dependencies and interdependencies

---

[3]DHS, *National Infrastructure Protection Plan* (Washington, D.C.: June 2006). DHS updated the NIPP in January 2009 to include a greater emphasis on resiliency. See DHS, *National Infrastructure Protection Plan, Partnering to Enhance Protection and Resiliency* (Washington, D.C.: January 2009).

[4]See, e.g., Pub. L. No. 107-296, § 201(d)(5), 116 Stat. 2135, 2146 (2002) (codified at 6 U.S.C. § 121(d)(5)). According to DHS, the NIPP risk management framework is a planning methodology that outlines the process for setting goals and objectives; identifying assets, systems, and networks; assessing risk based on consequences, vulnerabilities, and threats; implementing protective programs and resiliency strategies; and measuring performance and taking corrective action.

among the assets that participate in the RRAP, (2) cascading effects resulting from an all-hazards disruption of those assets or the region, (3) characteristics that make the assets and the region resilient, and (4) any resilience gaps that may hinder rapid recovery from disruptions.

RRAP projects are conducted by DHS officials; including DHS field representatives, called protective security advisors (PSA), in collaboration with SSAs; other federal officials; state, local, territorial, and tribal officials; and the private sector depending upon the sectors and assets selected. PSAs are to work with a primary stakeholder—generally officials representing the sponsoring state government—to develop project proposals and, among other things, perform outreach with various other stakeholders involved with the project.[5] They are to also schedule and conduct security surveys and vulnerability assessments at the assets included in the project and deliver the final RRAP product to the primary stakeholder.[6] The final product is a report that is to discuss various factors including any resilience gaps identified, and DHS suggestions, called resilience enhancement options, for addressing them. From fiscal year 2009 through fiscal year 2012, DHS conducted 27 RRAP projects in various locations throughout the country. These projects covered assets in various CI sectors, including what DHS calls lifeline sectors, a term used to refer to geographically distributed sectors—such as the energy, water, waste-water, and communications sectors—that provide essential support systems for the well-being and security of the communities they serve.

Given DHS's efforts to develop and implement the RRAP and its efforts to work with stakeholders to conduct RRAP projects, you asked that we examine DHS's overall management of the program. This report assesses the extent to which DHS

---

[5]For most RRAP projects, the sponsoring state was the primary stakeholder. In one instance, the Tennessee Valley Authority (TVA) was the primary stakeholder. For the purposes of this report, we refer to all other RRAP participants as stakeholders.

[6]DHS security surveys are intended to gather information on an asset's current security posture and overall security awareness. DHS vulnerability assessments are conducted during site visits at individual assets and are used to identify security gaps and provide options for consideration to mitigate these identified gaps. Security surveys and vulnerability assessments are generally asset-specific and are conducted at the request of asset owners and operators.

GAO-13-616 Critical Infrastructure Protection

- developed criteria for identifying RRAP project locations,

- worked with states to conduct RRAP projects and shared information with critical infrastructure partners to promote resilience, and

- is positioned to measure results associated with RRAP projects.

To address all of our objectives, we reviewed applicable laws, regulations, and directives as well as IP policies and procedures for conducting RRAP projects, providing their results, and assessing the effectiveness of this program. We also interviewed a sample of 10 state officials and 20 PSAs that have conducted RRAP projects for their perspectives on the RRAP process. Our sampling methodology for PSAs included all PSAs that conducted RRAP projects in 2011 (6) and 2012 (10) and 2 PSAs each from RRAP projects conducted in 2009 and 2010 (4 of the 11 RRAP projects conducted in those years), for a total of 20 PSAs.[7] We used a sample of PSAs for the 2009 and 2010 program years because the RRAP was considered a pilot program in those years, and DHS officials told us the process had changed a great deal by 2011. For our sample of state officials, we included four officials representing states where RRAP projects were performed in 2009 and 2010 where we spoke to PSAs, respectively, and officials representing all six RRAP projects completed during 2011 to obtain their perspectives on the RRAP process and the resulting RRAP report. We did not include state officials for the 2012 RRAP projects because these reports had not been issued at the time of our review, so these state officials would be unable to offer their perspectives on the value of the reports and the use of the results. While the results of the interviews are not generalizable, they provided insight into the importance and conduct of the program from the perspective of key RRAP participants.

To address our first objective, we reviewed key documents, including the 17 RRAP reports distributed since the program's inception in 2009.[8] Additionally, we analyzed DHS's RRAP selection records, where

---

[7]For our 2009 and 2010 PSA sample we used judgment and selected PSAs who had participated in RRAP projects each with a different sector focus. For 2009 we chose lifelines and energy RRAP projects and for 2010 transportation and commercial facilities RRAP projects.

[8]At the time of our review, reports had not been issued for the 10 RRAP projects initiated during fiscal year 2012.

available, to identify (1) the various factors DHS has considered when selecting RRAP locations since 2009 and (2) how DHS documented these decisions, if at all. We also interviewed IP officials as well as state officials to understand the process DHS uses to identify and select RRAP locations and sectors. We then compared the results of these steps against the criteria in the NIPP's risk management framework and federal internal control standards.[9] In addition to the DHS and state officials mentioned above, we also interviewed members of the State, Local, Tribal and Territorial Government Coordinating Council (SLTTGCC)—a cross-sector council that serves as a forum to ensure that state, local, and tribal homeland security partners are fully integrated as active participants in national CI protection efforts—to obtain their perspectives on the RRAP selection process. We also spoke to members of SLTTGCC's RRAP Working Group, which was formed to address member concerns about how DHS selects and conducts RRAP projects.

To answer our second objective, we reviewed prior GAO and DHS Office of Inspector General reports on CI protection coordination efforts. We analyzed all issued RRAP reports for RRAP projects conducted from 2009 through 2011 to help identify the roles of federal partners and states. We interviewed officials at DHS and officials representing Argonne National Laboratory (ANL), the contractor that works with DHS to conduct RRAP projects. We interviewed officials representing nine SSAs that DHS listed as having participated in RRAP projects or whose sectors were either the focus sector of a RRAP project or a key supporting sector based on our review of the issued RRAP reports.[10] We spoke with the

---

[9]GAO, *Standards for Internal Control in the Federal Government*, GAO/AIMD-00-21.3.1 (Washington, D.C.: Nov. 1, 1999). Internal control is an integral component of an organization's management that provides reasonable assurance that the following objectives are being achieved: effectiveness and efficiency of operations, reliability of financial reporting, and compliance with applicable laws and regulations. These standards, issued pursuant to the requirements of the Federal Managers' Financial Integrity Act of 1982 (FMFIA), provide the overall framework for establishing and maintaining internal control in the federal government. Also pursuant to FMFIA, the Office of Management and Budget issued Circular A-123, revised December 21, 2004, to provide the specific requirements for assessing the reporting on internal controls. Internal control standards and the definition of internal control in Circular A-123 are based on GAO's *Standards for Internal Control in the Federal Government*.

[10]The SSA sample included SSAs from the Office of Infrastructure Protection—chemical, commercial facilities, and dams; sectors managed by other DHS components—communications, information technology and transportation; and sectors managed by other agencies—energy, food and agriculture and water. See appendix I, table 2, for a list of SSAs and critical infrastructure sectors.

GAO-13-616 Critical Infrastructure Protection

chair of SLTTGCC and members of its RRAP Working Group to obtain the council's perspective regarding state and local concerns about the RRAP and DHS's actions taken to address these concerns. We interviewed officials from the states and PSAs to obtain their perspectives on the participation of federal and state stakeholders in RRAP projects and DHS's efforts to share information obtained from the RRAP projects with federal and state partners. We compared the results of our analysis with the partnering and information-sharing criteria in the NIPP and federal internal control standards and met with DHS officials to discuss any differences between stakeholder experiences and NIPP criteria, as well as to identify any opportunities to improve partnering and information sharing.[11]

To address our third objective, we reviewed DHS documentation on performance measures, including its Project Management Plan for vulnerability assessments and the RRAP *Findings Tracker* used by IP to gather RRAP data on activities related to, among other things, partnering and information sharing, and actions taken to address the findings of the RRAP report. We also interviewed DHS program officials to understand and describe the process through which DHS gathers data on actions taken to measure the impact of resilience changes resulting from the RRAP reports and obtain examples of efforts to measure performance, including guidelines and tools. In addition, we interviewed staff from ANL—the DHS contractor that compiles facility security survey and vulnerability assessment data—to discuss how resilience findings are developed. We also reviewed the NIPP and federal internal control standards and compared DHS's efforts to measure its performance with these standards. We identified any gaps in DHS's performance measurement approach, and met with DHS officials to determine why these gaps, if any, may have occurred and to discuss barriers, if any, to gathering and sharing performance measure information.

We conducted this performance audit from June 2012 to July 2013 in accordance with generally accepted government auditing standards. Those standards require that we plan and perform the audit to obtain sufficient, appropriate evidence to provide a reasonable basis for our findings and conclusions based on our audit objectives. We believe that

---

[11]GAO/AIMD-00-21.3.1.

the evidence obtained provides a reasonable basis for our findings and conclusions based on our audit objectives.

Background

DHS Roles and Responsibilities in Critical Infrastructure Protection

Various laws and directives guide DHS's role in critical infrastructure protection, including the Homeland Security Act of 2002, as amended,[12] the Homeland Security Presidential Directive/HSPD-7,[13] and most recently, Presidential Policy Directive/PPD-21, which was issued on February 12, 2013.[14] Consistent with HSPD-7, which directed DHS to establish uniform policies, approaches, guidelines, and methodologies for integrating federal infrastructure protection and risk management activities within and across CI sectors, 18 CI sectors were established. PPD-21, among other things, purports to refine and clarify critical infrastructure-related functions, roles, and responsibilities across the federal government, and enhance overall coordination and collaboration. Pursuant to PPD-21, which expressly revoked HSPD-7, 2 of the 18 sectors were incorporated into existing sectors, thereby reducing the number of CI sectors from 18 to 16 (app. I lists the CI sectors and their SSAs).[15]

PPD-21 directs DHS to, among other things, coordinate the overall federal effort to promote the security and resilience of the nation's critical infrastructure. PPD-21 also recognizes that DHS, in carrying out its responsibilities under the Homeland Security Act, evaluates national capabilities, opportunities, and challenges in protecting critical infrastructure; analyzes threats to, vulnerabilities of, and potential consequences from all hazards on critical infrastructure; identifies security

---

[12]See generally Pub. L. No. 107-296, 116 Stat. 2135 (2002). Title II of the Homeland Security Act, as amended, primarily addresses the department's responsibilities for critical infrastructure protection.

[13]Homeland Security Presidential Directive/HSPD-7—Critical Infrastructure Identification, Prioritization, and Protection (Washington, D.C.: Dec. 17, 2003).

[14]Presidential Policy Directive/PPD-21—*Critical Infrastructure Security and Resilience* (Washington, D.C.: Feb. 12, 2013).

[15]Although PPD-21 revoked HSPD-7, it further provides that any plans developed pursuant to HSPD-7 shall remain in effect until specifically revoked or superseded.

and resilience functions that are necessary for effective public-private engagement with all critical infrastructure sectors; and integrates and coordinates federal cross-sector security and resilience activities and identify and analyze key interdependencies among critical infrastructure sectors.

Within DHS, NPPD's IP is responsible for various activities intended to enhance CI protection and resilience across a number of sectors. While other entities may possess and exercise regulatory authority over CI to address security, such as for the chemical, transportation, and nuclear sectors, IP generally relies on voluntary efforts to secure CI because, in general, DHS has limited authority to directly regulate CI.[16] In carrying out its responsibilities, IP leads and coordinates national programs and policies on critical infrastructure issues and, among other things, conducts and facilitates security surveys and vulnerability assessments to help CI owners and operators and state, local, tribal, and territorial partners understand and address risks. In so doing, IP is responsible for working with public and private sector CI partners in the 16 sectors and leads the coordinated national effort to mitigate risk to the nation's CI through the development and implementation of CI protection and resilience programs.

IP's Protective Security Coordination Division (PSCD) provides programs and initiatives to enhance CI protection and resilience and reduce risk associated with all-hazards incidents. In so doing, PSCD works with CI owners and operators and state and local responders to (1) assess vulnerabilities, interdependencies, capabilities, and incident consequences; (2) develop, implement, and provide national coordination for protective programs; and (3) facilitate CI response to and recovery from incidents. Related to these efforts, PSCD has deployed 91 PSAs in 50 states and Puerto Rico, with deployment locations based on population density and major concentrations of CI. In these locations,

---

[16]Most of the nation's critical infrastructure is privately owned and does not fall within the regulatory scope of DHS or its components. Nonetheless, DHS components do regulate various CI sectors. For example, IP implements the Chemical Facility Anti-Terrorism Standards (CFATS) regulatory program, which establishes a risk-based approach to identifying and securing the nation's high-risk chemical facilities and manages the ammonium nitrate program. See 6 C.F.R. pt. 27 (Chemical Facility Anti-Terrorism Standards); 76 Fed. Reg. 46,908 (Aug. 3, 2011) (Ammonium Nitrate Security Program, proposed rule). IP's efforts with regard to CFATS and ammonium nitrate were outside the scope of this review.

PSAs are to act as the links between state, local, tribal, and territorial organizations and DHS infrastructure mission partners in the private sector and are to assist with ongoing state and local CI security efforts. PSAs are also to support the development of the national risk picture by conducting vulnerability and security assessments to identify security gaps and potential vulnerabilities in the nation's most critical infrastructures.[17] In addition, PSAs are to share vulnerability information and protective measure suggestions with local partners and asset owners and operators.

The Regional Resiliency Assessment Program

As discussed earlier, DHS developed the RRAP to assess vulnerability and risk associated with dependent and interdependent infrastructure clusters and systems in specific geographic areas. RRAP projects are intended to evaluate CI on a regional level to identify facilities and sectors that are dependent on one another, or interdependent. RRAP projects also identify situations where failures at facilities or sectors would lead to failures at other facilities or sectors, characteristics that make facilities and regions within the study resilient to disruptions, and resilience vulnerabilities that could promote or foster disruptions. According to DHS officials, the sectors selected to be studied as part of a RRAP project may vary based on priorities of IP and the state(s) where the RRAP occurs, that is, the "sector" focus can be narrow or broad, depending on the concerns of the state. For example, a transportation sector RRAP project in one state focused only on bridges, while another RRAP project in another state examined lifeline sectors.

The region or area covered by the RRAP project can also vary substantially. For example, the size of the "region" under study in a RRAP project in Colorado covered a few square miles within a city. Conversely,

---

[17]As part of their ongoing activities, PSAs are responsible for promoting the Enhanced Critical Infrastructure Protection (ECIP) Initiative, which includes a security survey, formally called the Infrastructure Survey Tool (IST). The PSA can use the IST to gather information on the asset's current security posture and overall security awareness on such topics as information sharing, security management, security force, protective measures, physical security, or dependencies. DHS also uses vulnerability assessments called site assistance visits (SAV) to identify security gaps and provide options for consideration to mitigate these identified gaps. These assessments are generally on-site and asset-specific and are conducted at the request of asset owners and operators. The results of the SAV are used to produce a report that includes options for consideration to increase an asset's ability to detect and prevent terrorist attacks and mitigation options that address the identified vulnerabilities of the asset.

another RRAP covered an entire industry spread across a large state and yet another RRAP is looking at infrastructure that crosses 12 states. Accordingly, RRAP projects have been conducted in various locations throughout the country covering a wide variety of CI sectors and regions. These RRAP projects include one covering the financial district in Chicago; three covering commercial facilities in cities like Minneapolis, Atlanta, and Las Vegas; and one covering energy production facilities managed by the Tennessee Valley Authority. Figure 1 provides a map showing the states where RRAP projects have been completed or are planned.[18]

---

[18]According to IP officials, DHS plans to conduct 10 RRAP projects in fiscal year 2013. Nine of these RRAP projects are new and the 10th is a regional pipeline RRAP project that was begun in fiscal year 2012.

Figure 1: National Map of Regional Resiliency Assessment Program (RRAP) Projects from Fiscal Years 2009 through 2013 (Planned)

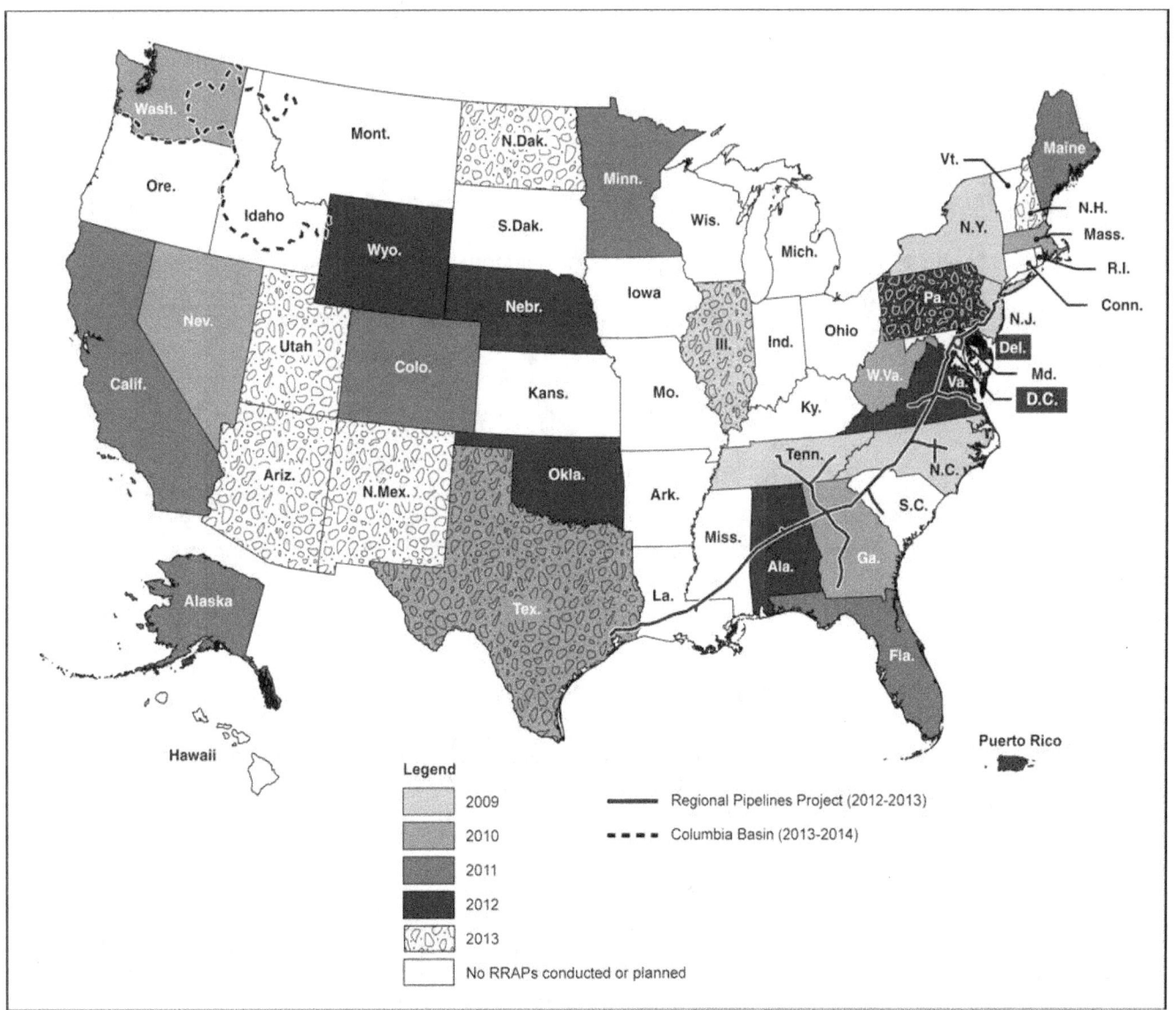

Source: GAO analysis of DHS data.

Note: Three states—Illinois, Texas, and Pennsylvania—have RRAPs planned for fiscal year 2013, but also had RRAPs conducted in fiscal years 2009, 2010, and 2012, respectively.

According to DHS officials, the current process for conducting a RRAP project can take from 18 to 24 months from start to finish. The process includes

- selecting and scoping RRAP projects from proposals;

- assembling and preparing a RRAP team of federal, state and local stakeholders;

- training the states via webinar (i.e., stakeholder awareness training);

- conducting an introductory kickoff (i.e., outreach) meeting;

- gathering preliminary data and selecting sites to be included in the review;

- scheduling meetings with asset owners or operators of the sites;

- conducting ongoing analyses using data derived from performing the aforementioned vulnerability and security assessments at facilities;[19]

- conducting stakeholders' meetings for training purposes and to discuss regional resilience issues;[20]

- preparing a draft report for state review;

- incorporating the state's feedback into a final report; and

- establishing a process to follow up with stakeholders to, among other things, periodically update their progress making RRAP-related enhancements.

---

[19]DHS uses security surveys and vulnerability assessments and other tools, such as cybersecurity resiliency reviews, at individual facilities. DHS uses the results of these reviews, among other things, to assess the interdependencies among the facilities covered and any gaps that may make these facilities vulnerable to disruptions during an all-hazards event.

[20]According to IP officials, these meetings are to include training and preparation for response to bombing incidents and discussions where public and private stakeholders examine their responsibilities, authorities, plans, policies, procedures, and resources required for responding to and recovering from a major event.

The final RRAP report typically includes a description of the key findings of the vulnerabilities in the sector(s) and region under study, including vulnerabilities for individual facilities, a hazard and risk analysis for the region and sector under review, and an analysis of dependencies and interdependencies. Also included in the RRAP report are resilience enhancement options that provide the report recipient suggestions to address key findings and mitigate the indentified vulnerability or weakness, and a list of organizations or funding sources that could provide the state and other stakeholders with support if they choose to implement an identified resilience enhancement option. RRAP reports can provide insights into the resilience of a region and the sector(s) under review and the gaps that could prompt regional disruptions.

Another aspect of the program centers on DHS's efforts to use RRAP projects to build stakeholder relationships and enhance information sharing and coordination among stakeholders in a particular region. For example, one RRAP report stated that fostering relationships between key facilities and supporting infrastructure providers was necessary to improve response to a hazard or incident. Another RRAP project sought to coordinate a partnership of key players and stakeholders (including both public and private sector stakeholders in the sector of focus and local law enforcement) to improve information sharing necessary for responding to a contamination in the food supply system. According to DHS officials, the creation and continuation of these stakeholder relationships is a major benefit of RRAP projects and the RRAP process. DHS officials said it is often the case that regional CI stakeholders were not acquainted and did not understand how their own operations were related to those of other stakeholders until the RRAP was conducted.

For fiscal year 2013, as in past fiscal years, the RRAP does not have a budget line item; rather the costs for the program are funded with resources budgeted for DHS's vulnerability assessment program and for PSAs. DHS officials estimated that the cost to PSCD for the average RRAP project is currently less than $1 million, including IP assessments, contractor support, and travel and administrative costs. The estimate does not include costs incurred for services rendered by other IP branches that participate in RRAP projects, like IP's National Infrastructure Simulation and Analysis Center (NISAC), which, among other things, develops computerized simulations of the effect of an all-hazards event on particular geographic areas. The estimate also does not include costs incurred by other SSAs, or the states and localities participating in a RRAP project.

DHS Has Developed Criteria to Identify RRAP Project Candidates, but Does Not Fully Document Its Project Recommendation and Selection Process

PSCD has developed criteria that consider various factors when selecting possible locations and sectors for RRAP projects. PSCD uses the criteria to develop lists of RRAP project candidates, and officials use this list to make final project selections. However, PSCD officials do not fully document why certain project candidates are or are not recommended for selection by the IP Assistant Secretary.

DHS's Approach for Identifying and Selecting RRAP Projects Has Evolved

IP's approach for identifying and selecting RRAP projects has evolved since the program's inception in 2009. For fiscal years 2009 and 2010, IP headquarters officials stated that they identified and selected RRAP project locations and sectors based on IP interests and preferences while considering input from primary stakeholders. IP officials told us that they relied heavily on IP's interests and preferences because they considered RRAP projects conducted during this time frame as pilot projects. For fiscal years 2011 and 2012, IP officials stated that they refined their process for identifying and selecting RRAP projects to incorporate more input from primary stakeholders. For example, IP officials developed a RRAP project template for PSAs and states to use when jointly developing RRAP project proposals. The template included information on regional characteristics and risk, the willingness of state and facility stakeholders to participate, potential outcomes of the RRAP analysis, and planning and logistical considerations. While considering project proposals states and PSAs jointly developed using the template, IP headquarters officials also developed their own RRAP project proposals (using open source documents for major metropolitan areas) to ensure IP leadership could consider a range of projects across a variety of sectors and locations. IP officials stated that when selecting projects during fiscal years 2011 and 2012, they considered, among other factors, information obtained from the template and, if applicable, risk-based factors such as the concentration of critical infrastructure, and IP management judgment as to the feasibility of conducting the project.

More recently, for projects planned to begin in fiscal year 2013, IP took two actions to further revise its RRAP project identification and selection process. First, IP revised its process from that used in previous years by considering only RRAP project proposals submitted jointly by PSAs and states. According to IP officials, they made this change to help ensure that RRAP locations and sectors reflected state priorities, particularly in light of lessons learned from past RRAP projects and feedback from SLTTGCC. In a 2011 report on state and local government CI resilience activities, SLTTGCC expressed, among other things, concern about the scope of RRAP projects—particularly when states did not request the RRAP project—and the cost and resources required to be involved in a RRAP project.

Second, IP officials developed nine point selection criteria to identify lists of potential RRAP project candidates. IP officials stated that they developed the criteria to help evaluate proposals and to develop lists of potential candidate projects given the volume of proposals generated by states and PSAs and the DHS resources available to conduct RRAP projects. IP officials told us that they asked PSAs and PSA regional directors who had previously conducted RRAP projects to review the criteria before the criteria were finalized to provide assurance that the criteria reflected lessons learned.

Our review of IP criteria shows that it focuses on nine questions in four broad categories: whether the proposed project (1) is feasible, (2) promotes partnering with important stakeholders, (3) will produce results with broad applicability to other locations, and (4) accounts for risk-based factors. These criteria were used to evaluate the RRAP project proposals used to make the fiscal year 2013 and 2014 RRAP project recommendations. Table 1 lists the criteria IP uses to develop a list of feasible RRAP project candidates. A more detailed explanation of these criteria can be found in app. II, table 3.

Table 1: DHS Criteria for Identifying Candidate Regional Resiliency Assessment Program Projects, Fiscal Years 2013 and 2014

Feasibility	Does the proposed project clearly relate to regional infrastructure resilience and the Office of Infrastructure Protection's mission?
	Is the project concept sound?
Partnering	Does the proposed project have a clearly identified primary stakeholder that is willing and able to participate (e.g., such as a state)?
	Does the proposed project have clearly identified and willing participants (e.g., such as critical infrastructure owners and operators)?
Broad applicability	Does the proposed project have the potential to contribute to a larger resilience picture or applicability beyond the focus area?
Risk-based factors	Is the proposed project likely to produce original key findings and resilience enhancement options?
	Is there a plausible and compelling disruption, vulnerability, consequence story—the negative impact of an incident on the region—associated with the proposed project's focus?[a]
	Are resilience enhancement options likely to be implemented?
	Does the proposed geographic area meet the threshold (to be established each year) of concentration of critical infrastructure?

Source: GAO analysis of DHS information.

[a]According to the *National Infrastructure Protection Plan*, disruptions refer to the cascading effects resulting from an incident, such as an attack or natural disaster, on critical infrastructure assets, systems, or networks.

According to officials, IP analysts use the nine criteria to develop a list of RRAP project candidates by comparing project proposals against the criteria and developing a score for each project. To develop a score for each proposal, an individual IP analyst creates a checklist across the nine criteria to determine the overall feasibility of conducting a RRAP project. The individual analysts then review proposals and assign a one or a zero to each of the nine criteria depending on whether they believe the proposal or supplemental information gathered sufficiently supports each factor.[21] A score of one indicates that the proposal met the criterion; thus a proposal where all criteria were met would score a nine. Once all proposals have been scored, a group of IP analysts convene to discuss the scores across the nine criteria and may amend scores based on those discussions. Project candidates that receive a score of seven or

[21]DHS analysts may conduct supplemental research or contact PSAs or state officials to gather additional information. For example, to determine whether the proposed project is likely to produce original key findings and resiliency enhancement options, the analyst may reach out to the PSA and other critical infrastructure stakeholders to see if the state or other organization has initiated similar work to avoid duplicative activities.

above are then referred to PSCD officials for further consideration, and PSCD officials select among those candidates to develop a list of recommended projects for approval by the IP Assistant Secretary.[22] Figure 2 depicts IP's current RRAP proposal and selection process, as of May 2013.

Figure 2: DHS's Regional Resiliency Assessment Program (RRAP) Proposal and Selection Process as of May 2013

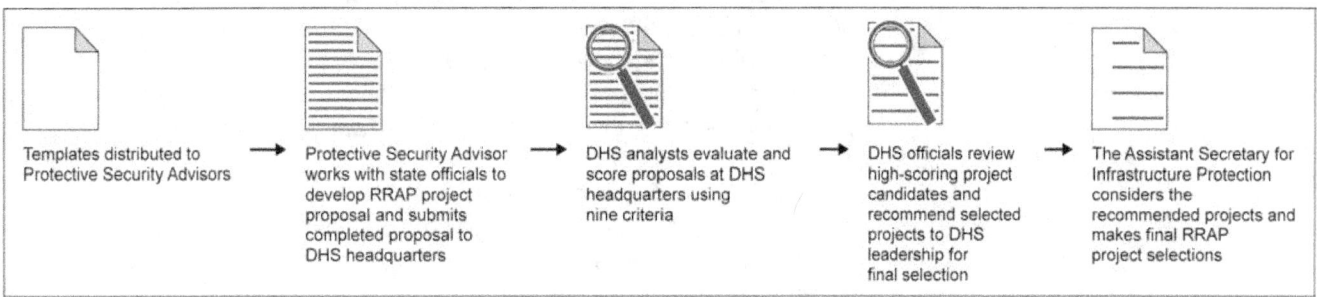

Templates distributed to Protective Security Advisors → Protective Security Advisor works with state officials to develop RRAP project proposal and submits completed proposal to DHS headquarters → DHS analysts evaluate and score proposals at DHS headquarters using nine criteria → DHS officials review high-scoring project candidates and recommend selected projects to DHS leadership for final selection → The Assistant Secretary for Infrastructure Protection considers the recommended projects and makes final RRAP project selections

Source: GAO analysis of DHS information.

DHS Does Not Fully Document Its RRAP Project Recommendation and Selection Process

According to PSCD officials, the Assistant Secretary for IP selects projects from among those candidates PSCD officials recommend, but PSCD officials did not fully document why specific project candidates were or were not recommended for selection. For fiscal years 2013 and 2014, IP analysts identified 22 project candidates that scored a seven or greater. PSCD officials stated that after further review, they recommended that the Assistant Secretary select 16 of the 22 projects— 10 to be conducted in fiscal year 2013 and 6 to be conducted in fiscal year 2014.[23] For fiscal year 2013, the IP Assistant Secretary selected all 10 of PSCD's recommended project candidates. According to PSCD officials, the Assistant Secretary plans to make final fiscal year 2014 project selections in October 2013. For the 16 projects, IP officials told us

---

[22]According to IP officials, in fiscal year 2013, they established a score of seven as the threshold for considering project candidates. These officials said that the threshold was established based on a review of that year's scoring data. IP officials stated that they expect that the threshold will change from year to year depending on the number and relative strength (i.e., scores) of RRAP proposals submitted for consideration.

[23]According to DHS officials, 1 of the 10 projects selected for fiscal year 2013 will be the second year of the multiyear Regional Pipelines RRAP project that began in fiscal year 2012 and 1 of the 6 projects recommended for fiscal year 2014 will be the second year of the multiyear Columbia Basin RRAP project that began in fiscal year 2013.

they provided the Assistant Secretary information about each of the recommended project candidates. However, PSCD officials did not document why individual projects were recommended over others, including candidate projects that received the same score—they stated that they believe providing such information on the projects that are recommended is sufficient. For example, 1 of the fiscal year 2014 candidate projects recommended to the Assistant Secretary—a health care sector project in New Jersey—had a score of seven. By contrast, 3 other potential candidates—1 food and agriculture sector project in Pennsylvania, a transportation sector project in South Carolina, and a lifeline sector project in the U.S. Virgin Islands—each scored an eight, and none were recommended to the Assistant Secretary for selection.

Although PSCD officials did not provide documentation, PSCD officials explained that there can be a variety of reasons why they recommend that the Assistant Secretary select 1 RRAP project over another—including geographic and sector diversity, IP's strategic priorities, and the availability of PSCD resources. Additionally, PSCD officials provided examples of why some projects were recommended over others. For example, PSCD officials told us that one PSA had submitted three separate proposals, all of which received scores of seven or above, but PSCD recommended only one of the three for selection by the Assistant Secretary because a PSA can participate in only one RRAP at a time. In another case, PSCD officials told us that an international partner for a cross-border transportation project could not participate because of resource constraints. However, without documentation, we were unable to determine why PSCD recommended 1 project candidate that scored a seven over the 3 other potential candidates that scored an eight.

Standards for Internal Control in the Federal Government states that all transactions and significant events should be promptly recorded to maintain their relevance and value to management in controlling operations and making decisions. The standards further call for all transactions and significant events to be clearly documented, and readily available for examination to inform decision making.[24] Recording and documenting key decisions are among the suite of control activities that are an essential part of an agency's planning, implementing, and reviewing, and they are essential for proper stewardship and

---

[24]GAO/AIMD-00-21.3.1.

accountability for government resources and achieving efficient and effective program results. Documenting the rationale for making project selections would provide DHS managers and others responsible for overseeing the program valuable insights into why 1 RRAP project was selected over another, particularly among proposals with the same score that appear equally feasible and worthy. DHS officials agreed that maintaining this documentation could be used to support the recommendations and help answer any potential questions about final project selections.

Maintaining documentation about reasons why projects were or were not selected would also provide DHS a basis for defending its selections or responding to queries about them, particularly given the desirability of the program among the states and budgetary constraints facing states and other potential RRAP stakeholders. Regarding the budgetary constraints, states or other stakeholders, such as local, tribal, or territorial government entities, might be interested in knowing why a RRAP project proposal was not selected so that they could make decisions about (1) whether they need to dedicate additional resources to refining a RRAP proposal for future years, or (2) adjust the scope of their involvement in a future RRAP based on anticipated budgetary resource increases or constraints. With documentation on why projects were or were not recommended and selected, DHS would be better positioned to respond to queries about project selections from potential RRAP stakeholders, particularly if senior managers or staff currently involved in the program move to other positions and new managers or staff do not have records about key decisions.

DHS Has Taken Action to Work with States to Improve the RRAP Process, and Has Begun to Engage CI Partners to Ascertain Their Resilience Information Needs

Since 2011, IP has worked with states to improve the RRAP process, and IP officials said these efforts are viewed favorably by primary stakeholders. IP shares the project results of each RRAP with the primary stakeholder, and each report is generally available to IP staff, including PSAs and SSAs within IP, but IP does not share individual reports with others, including other primary stakeholders and SSAs outside of DHS. According to IP officials, IP has begun to conceptualize how it can develop a resilience product or products using multiple sources— including RRAP reports—to distribute to CI partners, and is using various forums to solicit input from CI partners to gauge their resilience information needs.

DHS Has Responded to Concerns Raised by States and Worked with the States to Improve the RRAP Process

In May 2011, SLTTGCC expressed concerns about states being selected to conduct a RRAP project before first being provided information on the time, cost, and scope of conducting a RRAP project.[25] SLTTGCC established its RRAP Working Group in September 2011 in response to states' experiences participating in the RRAP in fiscal years 2009 and 2010, with the goal to help ensure that other states had better experiences with DHS in future RRAP projects. In addition, some RRAP project participants we interviewed told us that maintaining the RRAP project schedule had been a challenge. Specifically, officials representing 5 of the 10 primary stakeholders we contacted in locations where RRAP projects had taken place from fiscal years 2009 through 2011 told us that they had encountered challenges completing RRAP projects within a specific time frame. Moreover, 12 of the 20 PSAs we contacted agreed that it was challenging to schedule meetings, such as kickoff meetings that required all key stakeholders to be in the same room during the meetings. Six of these PSAs also said it was challenging to get all required surveys and assessments completed in the short (usually 2 months) data-gathering period.

IP officials told us that they took actions to address these challenges by improving communication with participants about the scope of RRAP projects before they were selected and while projects were ongoing. These officials stated that this included setting expectations early on to inform stakeholders when particular RRAP events are scheduled to occur, including scheduling vulnerability assessments, and group discussions among the various stakeholders participating in the RRAP. Officials representing two of the four primary stakeholders that participated in the fiscal year 2009 or 2010 RRAP projects and were active in SLTTGCC stated that they believed IP has improved the conduct of later projects. One of these state officials said including states in the proposal development process and helping states to understand the time, costs, and benefit of the RRAP project prior to initiating the project made the execution of RRAP projects go more smoothly. IP officials told us that that they have since received positive feedback from the states regarding these changes, and our discussions with a representative of SLTTGCC confirmed that they believe that DHS's revised proposal development process had been beneficial to them.

---

[25]SLTTGCC, *Federal Critical Infrastructure Programs Review: Next Steps*, May 2011.

DHS Shares RRAP Project Results with Primary Stakeholders and Some Partners, but Relies on the Primary Stakeholder for Broader Distribution

IP shares individual RRAP reports with the primary stakeholders—officials representing the state where the RRAP was conducted—but has generally limited the distribution of the reports to those officials. According to IP, individual RRAP project reports are provided directly to primary stakeholders. PSAs and others that have access to the IP Gateway may also view RRAP reports.[26] When the RRAP report contains Protected Critical Infrastructure Information (PCII), distribution and access to those reports is limited to individuals that are authorized to receive such information.[27] Upon the request of a primary stakeholder, IP will also prepare For Official Use Only (FOUO) versions of RRAP reports—which, although sensitive, may be shared with a broader audience than PCII versions—to share with primary stakeholders.[28] When this occurs, IP develops FOUO and PCII versions of RRAP reports—and primary stakeholders can share FOUO results with whomever they deem appropriate or necessary, including other RRAP participants. Otherwise, to share information within PCII reports, states would need to identify the FOUO information within the PCII report or request that IP clear the recipient for access to PCII information. During our review, 13 of 17

[26]The IP Gateway, formerly known as the Link Encrypted Network System (LENS), hosts IP's facility database, which records, among other things, records of IP's assessments and other interactions with facilities. The IP Gateway portal is restricted and allows authorized users to obtain, post, and exchange information and access common resources, particularly critical infrastructure information, including security survey data.

[27]In general, Protected Critical Infrastructure Information (PCII) is validated Critical Infrastructure Information (CII)—that is, information not customarily in the public domain and related to the security of critical infrastructure or protected systems—that is voluntarily submitted, directly or indirectly, to DHS for its use regarding the security of critical infrastructure and protected systems, analysis, warning, interdependency study, recovery, reconstitution, or other appropriate purpose. See 6 C.F.R. § 29.2(b), (g). Pursuant to the Critical Infrastructure Information (CII) Act of 2002, DHS established the PCII program to institute a means to facilitate the voluntary sharing of critical infrastructure information with the federal government by providing assurances of safeguarding and limited disclosure. See 6 U.S.C. §§ 131-34; see also 6 C.F.R. pt. 29 (implementing the CII Act through the establishment of uniform procedures for the receipt, care, and storage of voluntarily submitted CII). Consistent with its implementing regulations, the PCII Program Office is responsble for, among other things, validating information provided by CI partners as PCII and developing protocols to access and safeguard all that is deemed PCII.

[28]According to DHS, *For Official Use Only* (FOUO) is used to identify unclassified information of a sensitive nature, not otherwise categorized by statute or regulation, the unauthorized disclosure of which could adversely affect a person's privacy or welfare, the conduct of federal programs, or other programs or operations essential to the national interest. See Department of Homeland Security Management Directive Number 11042.1, *Safeguarding Sensitive but Unclassified (For Official Use Only) Information* (Jan. 6, 2005).

RRAP projects had both PCII and FOUO versions of RRAP reports, the other 4 projects had PCII versions only. IP officials told us that state officials can share FOUO versions of RRAP reports more readily than PCII versions of the reports. Furthermore, PSAs told us they share RRAP-derived information with CI partners—both those who participated in the RRAP and those who did not—during the course of their PSA duties as appropriate. IP officials told us that they do not distribute non-PCII versions of RRAP reports more broadly because the individual state is the primary stakeholder for a particular RRAP report. They said that they consider the state to be the owner of the information and believe that any party who wants the information should go to the state. Officials said they provide point-of-contact information for the primary stakeholder of a particular RRAP project to those who want to request a RRAP report from that primary stakeholder.

IP does not proactively distribute RRAP reports to SSAs whose sectors are the focus of the RRAP project. Officials representing the eight of nine SSAs we contacted told us they do not generally receive RRAP reports and may be unaware the reports exist. Representatives of two SSAs stated that they did not know about the existence of certain RRAP reports for their sector, and officials representing two others told us they made multiple requests before receiving RRAP reports from DHS. IP officials stated that SSAs should be able to receive a copy of any RRAP report in which they participated and stated that it was possible that we did not speak to the appropriate SSA representatives—those that participated in the RRAP projects. IP officials also stated that RRAP reports are on the IP Gateway and IP SSAs—chemical, commercial facilities, critical manufacturing, dams, emergency services, and nuclear sectors—have access to these reports, but other SSAs may have to make specific requests to IP or the primary stakeholder in order to receive the RRAP reports because not all of these SSAs have access to the IP Gateway and PCII information. IP officials told us that they intend to share a FOUO copy of a RRAP report on regional energy pipelines with the non-IP SSAs who participated. IP officials stated that the regional energy pipelines RRAP project is not expected to be completed until the latter part of 2013.

DHS Plans to Develop an Approach to Share Resilience Information and Has Engaged CI Partners to Ascertain Their Information Needs

IP is in the early stages of developing an approach—either a product or a series of products—to share resilience-related lessons learned, but plans are in the early concept stage and few specifics are available regarding the contents of these products. According to IP officials, the planned product or products are not to be limited to RRAP project data or findings. Rather they will leverage RRAP data and common observations or findings; data from security surveys and vulnerability assessments done at individual assets or facilities; and open source information to communicate collective results, lessons learned, and best practices that can contribute to ongoing local, state, regional, and national efforts to strengthen the resilience of critical infrastructure systems. IP officials anticipate that the first product, or products, will be available for distribution before the end of fiscal year 2013.

With regard to the planned resilience product(s), IP officials cautioned that (1) this effort is in the conceptual stage, (2) DHS has not approved funding for the product(s), and (3) the product or products are not expected to be ready for distribution until later this year at the earliest. IP officials further stated that it is too early to determine whether this approach will be an effective means to share resilience information across the spectrum of CI partners, to include states and SSAs. Nonetheless, IP officials told us that they engage CI partners, such as SLTTGCC's RRAP and information-sharing working groups on resilience and information sharing, and during their participation in sector agency meetings and private sector coordination council meetings where, according to officials, the views of SSAs and CI owners and operators are discussed. For example, IP officials said they have had specific discussions with CI partners concerning state resilience information needs, and they are considering this input as they begin to develop a resilience product or products. They said that they also are considering feedback on information needs that they receive at regional conferences attended by various CI partners, and during daily PSA contacts in the field, primarily with CI owners and operators.

IP's efforts to solicit feedback from CI partners during development of any resilience information-sharing product or products is consistent with the NIPP, which states that when the government is provided with an understanding of information needs, it can adjust its information collection, analysis, synthesis, and sharing accordingly. Through outreach and engagement with CI partners, DHS should be better positioned to understand their needs for information about resilience practices. It also helps DHS clarify the scope of work needed to develop a meaningful resilience information-sharing product or products that are useful across sectors and assets, and ascertain how the information can best be disseminated to the various CI partners—issues that could be critical given current budgetary constraints and uncertainty over the availability of resources.

DHS Gathers Facility Data, but Faces Challenges Measuring Results of RRAP Projects

PSCD uses follow-up surveys at facilities that have undergone vulnerability assessments and security surveys, including those that participate in RRAP projects, and has initiated a broad data-gathering effort with its RRAP CI stakeholders to explore changes in diverse topics such as partnering and state actions based on RRAP participation. These are important steps to provide insight about RRAP projects, but PSCD faces challenges developing performance measures and is not positioned to gauge the RRAP's impact on regional resilience.

DHS Gathers Data on Resilience Enhancements at Individual Facilities

According to the NIPP, the use of performance measures is a critical step in the risk management process to enable DHS to objectively and quantitatively assess improvement in CI protection and resilience at the sector and national levels. The NIPP states that the use of performance metrics provides a basis for DHS to establish accountability, document actual performance, promote effective management, and provide a feedback mechanism to decision makers.

IP gathers data from individual facilities, including those that participated in RRAP projects, with the intent of measuring the efforts of those facilities to make enhancements arising out of security surveys and vulnerability assessments performed during RRAP projects. As discussed earlier, PSAs support the development of the national risk picture by conducting vulnerability assessments and security surveys to identify security gaps and potential vulnerabilities in the nation's most critical infrastructure. PSAs perform these surveys and assessments at individual assets and facilities, including those that participate in RRAP projects, across the 16 sectors. In January 2011, IP directed PSAs to follow up with security survey and vulnerability assessment participants to gather feedback on security and resilience enhancements at their facilities using standardized data collection tools. These follow-up tools were to be used by PSAs to ask asset representatives about enhancements in six general categories—information sharing, security management, security force, protective measures, physical security, and dependencies—and focused on changes made directly as a result of IP security surveys and vulnerability assessments.

According to IP officials, PSCD revised its security survey and vulnerability assessment in January 2013 to include additional resilience-related questions intended to focus on facility preparedness, mitigation measures, response capabilities, and recovery mechanisms among facilities that participated in a security survey or vulnerability assessment. In addition, officials said beginning after July 2013, facilities that received a survey or assessment using the revised resilience questions are also to receive a PSA follow-up visit that reflects those same updated questions. IP officials said that revisions to the follow-up tools will also reflect changes associated with security and resilience enhancements at the facility, distinguishing them as either security or resilience changes. Officials said security surveys and vulnerability assessments that were conducted on facilities in support of a RRAP project are noted as such in the IP Gateway, but there is no other additional or separate tracking for the purposes of performance metrics. Furthermore, officials said they continue to gather data on changes initiated at facilities that participated in the RRAP, but they believe it may not be possible to link any changes made at facilities to participation in the RRAP. They added that resilience improvements made at individual facilities do not necessarily address regional vulnerabilities identified in RRAP reports.

DHS Faces Challenges Measuring the Effect of RRAP Projects

IP has considered how it intends to measure results associated with RRAP projects—not just facilities within projects— but faces challenges doing so. In January 2012, IP developed a project management plan (PMP) intended to clarify planned performance metrics for IP's vulnerability assessment programs, including the voluntary security surveys and vulnerability assessments performed during RRAP projects. The PMP stated that DHS planned to measure the impact of RRAP projects by conducting follow-up checks at RRAP facilities to see if these facilities or systems implemented changes that increased the resilience of the facility. The PMP set a goal of 20 percent of facilities making resilience improvements following a security survey or vulnerability assessment performed for RRAP projects for fiscal year 2013, rising to 50 percent of facilities by fiscal year 2017. The PMP stated that this facility information is to be used to compile resilience information for the region, but it did not explain how this information would be combined to measure regional resilience. In April 2013, IP officials told us that they no longer intended to use the performance targets contained in the PMP. IP officials explained that they believe that individual facility assessment follow-ups are not an effective means to measure the impact of a RRAP project. They said that RRAP findings are written for the primary stakeholder—the state and not the assessed facilities—and RRAP projects most often provide the analyses of larger regional issues rather than specific facility gaps.

Alternatively, PSCD officials stated that they have since developed the *RRAP Findings Tracker* to engage primary stakeholders about their efforts to address key findings resulting from individual RRAP projects. According to PSCD officials, in March 2013, the *RRAP Findings Tracker* was distributed to all PSAs who had conducted a RRAP project over the previous 3 years. PSAs were directed by IP to use the *RRAP Findings Tracker* to follow up with the state and other stakeholders on specific RRAP issues identified in those states. IP updates the tracker on a monthly basis and headquarters officials are to review the results every 6 months. The *RRAP Findings Tracker* is intended to cover, among other things:

- developments that demonstrate project relevance since the RRAP project was initiated, for instance, news reports, speeches, or studies that demonstrate the ongoing relevance of the project's focus;

- partnership building and information sharing, to include developments that relate to how project stakeholders—whether state, regional, federal, or private sector—have enhanced interaction, awareness, communication, and information sharing;

- any action taken concerning the RRAP report's key findings, particularly with regard to enhancement options specified in the RRAP report; and

- activities at specific individual assets assessed during the RRAP and their efforts to enhance resilience, including the percentage of assessed assets that have made an improvement or planned to make an improvement after 6 and 12 months.

PSCD officials said that they believe that by utilizing the information in its *Findings Tracker*, they would likely have greater insights into the extent that stakeholders take action following a RRAP project, such as the extent to which the project has improved communication among RRAP stakeholders. According to officials, in May 2013, they began having preliminary discussions about using the *RRAP Findings Tracker* as one input for developing possible metrics. They added that it would be would be premature for them to provide us with any of the preliminary draft ideas for metrics associated with this effort.

Nonetheless, IP officials also stated they face challenges measuring performance across facilities within a RRAP project, and from project to project. For example, IP officials told us that each RRAP project is difficult to measure because each focuses on unique assets within a unique geographic area or region. For example, our reviews of RRAP reports showed one RRAP project might focus on commercial facilities, such as stadiums and arenas in one urban area, while another project might focus on a shopping district or an urban mall in another. Similarly, a transportation RRAP project in one region may focus on roadways and bridges, while a project in a different region might focus on waterways. IP officials added that participation in a RRAP project is voluntary, as is participation in the completion of the *RRAP Findings Tracker*. Therefore, the ability to develop measures that represent assets in a region could hinge on the willingness of CI stakeholders, including facility owners and operators, to participate.

IP officials further explained that, given the diversity of assets and regions covered by individual RRAP projects, it could also be challenging to link key RRAP findings and subsequent actions within projects. For example, one RRAP project may identify a planning shortfall, leading to a resilience-enhancing option calling for the creation of a plan. If the affected stakeholder or stakeholders subsequently create such a plan, IP could note that an action or actions were taken toward addressing a key finding, but it would be unable to assess whether the plan addresses the key finding adequately until it was implemented and tested through an exercise or real-world emergency. Reaching that next step may take years, according to officials. Officials also stated that it might be difficult to develop measures of key findings across RRAP projects. Whereas a key finding of one RRAP project might focus on the development of a regional plan as discussed above, a key finding of another might focus on prioritizing the distribution on resources, such as fuel, to ensure that emergency services can remain viable during a hurricane or earthquake. A separate RRAP project might have a key finding that electrical power is provided by single supplier, leaving a region vulnerable to a single point of failure.

We recognize that developing performance measures among and across RRAP projects could be challenging moving forward. We further recognize that the information generated through the administration of the *RRAP Findings Tracker* with RRAP project primary stakeholders (e.g., states) may provide a foundation for DHS's development of RRAP performance measures. However, DHS could better position itself to gain insights into a project's effects if it were to develop a mechanism to

GAO-13-616 Critical Infrastructure Protection

assess whether changes made at individual facilities are linked to or influenced by participation in a RRAP project. One approach for doing so could entail IP revising its security survey and vulnerability assessment follow-up process at individual facilities, including follow-ups at facilities that participated in RRAP projects to gather and analyze data on the extent to which participation in a RRAP project influenced owners and operators to make related resilience enhancements. More specifically, IP officials stated earlier that they did believe it was possible to link security and resilience enhancements made at facilities that participated in RRAP projects to RRAP project participation. However, currently the PSA does not specifically ask facility owners and operators whether participation in the RRAP project influenced their enhancement decisions. Developing a mechanism—such as revising the security survey and vulnerability assessment follow-up tool—to ascertain whether changes made at individual facilities are linked to or influenced by findings in RRAP projects could provide IP valuable information on individual facility efforts to address key RRAP project findings and how any enhancements are linked to the RRAP project. Doing so would also enable IP to compare facilities that participated in a RRAP project with those that did not and provide a basis for assessing why RRAP participation may or may not have prompted changes at a facility, thereby providing a building block for measuring IP's performance and insights into the effect a RRAP project may have on facility resilience. This would also be consistent with the NIPP, which states that the use of performance metrics provides a basis for DHS to establish accountability, document actual performance, promote effective management, and provide feedback to decision makers.

Gathering data on the extent to which participation in a RRAP project influenced facility enhancements might also provide DHS valuable information about the results of its efforts, consistent with the views of PSAs who coordinate RRAP projects among stakeholders in particular regions. For example, 6 of the 10 PSAs we interviewed who had participated in RRAP projects where RRAP reports were issued expressed the belief that facilities that participated in the RRAP are more likely to have made improvements that increased security or resilience than other facilities that were not part of a RRAP project, but had undergone a security survey or assessment. These PSAs said that they believed this would occur because facilities participating in RRAP projects are able to see how their own operations affect the security and resilience of other facilities within the region. IP officials stated that they agreed that understanding whether RRAP participation had an effect on whether enhancements were made at an individual facility could provide useful information to the program. By assessing the linkage between the actions of individual facilities and the results of a RRAP project, DHS would also have a basis to begin to explore the effect of a RRAP project on facility management and operations, especially since RRAP projects are intended to focus on dependencies and interdependencies among facilities in a particular region.

Conclusions

IP has taken important actions to standardize the selection process for RRAP project locations. It has also worked with state stakeholders to better communicate the scope of projects, consider how it can share resilience information with CI partners, and gather information on CI partner actions to enhance resilience after the RRAP project is completed. However, further actions could strengthen these endeavors. First, with regard to the process for selecting RRAP project locations, IP has developed criteria and a process for selecting project candidates, but it has not fully documented why some projects are recommended over others. Documenting why specific RRAP selections were or were not recommended would be consistent with *Standards for Internal Control in the Federal Government*, and would provide IP managers and others responsible for overseeing the program valuable insights into why one RRAP project was selected over another, particularly among proposals with the same score that appear equally feasible and worthy. Furthermore, maintaining documentation about reasons why projects were or were not recommended would also provide IP a basis for defending its selections or responding to queries about them, particularly given the desirability of the program among the states and budgetary constraints facing states and other potential RRAP stakeholders. With documentation on why projects were or were not recommended and selected, DHS would be better positioned to respond to queries about project selections from potential RRAP stakeholders, particularly if senior managers or staff currently involved in the program move to other positions and new managers or staff do not have records about key decisions.

Second, consistent with the NIPP, IP has taken action to establish an approach for conducting follow-up surveys at facilities that have undergone security surveys and vulnerability assessments—both those that participated in RRAP projects and those that did not—to document changes the facilities make that affect their resilience. Also, IP has taken preliminary steps, via its *RRAP Findings Tracker*, to gain insights into primary stakeholder efforts to enhance resilience in the regions where RRAP projects have been performed. We recognize that IP faces challenges developing performance measures to gauge results among and across RRAP projects; nevertheless, IP could benefit from assessing how participation in a RRAP project may or may not influence change. Specifically, although the *RRAP Findings Tracker* may provide a foundation for IP's overall development of RRAP performance measures, IP could develop a mechanism to assess whether changes made at individual facilities are linked to or influenced by participation in a RRAP project. One such mechanism could entail IP revising its security survey and vulnerability assessment follow-up tool, which is used to query all facilities that have participated in these surveys and assessments— regardless of whether they participated in a RRAP project. Doing so would enable IP to compare the extent to which facilities that participated in a RRAP project made enhancements related to DHS security surveys and assessments with those that did not participate in a RRAP project. This comparison could serve as a building block for measuring IP's efforts to conduct RRAP projects, thereby providing an avenue to use performance metrics to establish accountability, document actual performance, promote effective management, and provide feedback to decision makers as stated in the NIPP. It would also provide valuable insights on individual facility efforts to address key RRAP findings, and give IP a basis for determining how those finding may have affected facility resilience, particularly as it relates to facility dependence and interdependence.

Recommendations for Executive Action

To help ensure that DHS is taking steps to strengthen the management of RRAP projects and the program in general, we recommend that the Assistant Secretary for Infrastructure Protection, Department of Homeland Security, take the following two actions:

- document decisions made with regard to recommendations about individual RRAP projects to provide insights into why one project was recommended over another and assurance that recommendations among equally feasible proposals are defensible, and

- develop a mechanism to assess the extent to which individual projects influenced participants to make RRAP related enhancements, such as revising the security and vulnerability assessment follow-up tool to query facilities that participated in RRAP projects on the extent to which any resilience improvements made are due to participation in the RRAP.

Agency Comments and Our Evaluation

We provided a draft of this report to the Secretary of Homeland Security for review and comment. DHS provided written comments, which are summarized below and reprinted in appendix III. DHS agreed with both recommendations and discussed plans to address one of them. DHS also provided technical comments, which we incorporated as appropriate.

With regard to the first recommendation, that DHS document decisions made with regard to recommendations about individual projects, DHS concurred, stating that the Office of Infrastructure Protection (IP) will develop a mechanism to more comprehensively document the decision-making process and justifications that lead to the selection of each project. DHS stated that it estimates that it will complete this action as of September 30, 2014, for projects in the next RRAP cycle—that is, projects to be conducted in fiscal year 2015.

With regard to the second recommendation, that DHS develop a mechanism, such as revising the security survey and vulnerability assessment follow-up tool, to assess the extent to which individual projects influenced participants to make RRAP related enhancements, DHS also concurred. In its written comments, DHS agreed that it would be insightful to understand whether the implementation rate of security and resilience enhancements at facilities differs between those receiving an assessment as part of a RRAP, and those receiving an assessment unrelated to this program. After we provided a draft of this report to DHS for review and comment, IP officials raised concerns that the recommendation as originally worded did not provide them the flexibility they needed to consider multiple alternatives to gain insights about RRAP-related enhancements. For example, and as noted in the written comments, facilities participate in the RRAP in many ways and surveys and assessments are but one option offered to facilities in a focus area. While we continue to see benefits to revising the security survey and vulnerability assessment follow-up tool, as discussed in the report, we modified the recommendation to acknowledge IP's concerns about considering other possible mechanisms. In its written comments, DHS stated that IP would review alternatives, including the one we discussed, and would provide additional details on how it will address this recommendation in DHS's written statement of the actions taken on our recommendations 60 calendar days after the receipt of the final report.[29] DHS stated that its estimated completion date for action on this recommendation is to be determined.

DHS also raised two concerns with the report. First, while concurring with our second recommendation, DHS stated that it is disappointed that the draft report did not have a more extensive discussion on the overall success and effectiveness of the RRAP to identify and address regional security and resilience gaps. DHS noted that since the RRAP's inception, projects have been conducted in regions throughout the nation and have focused on sectors such as energy, transportation, commercial facilities, water, and food and agriculture. DHS stated that through the RRAP, DHS has provided unique technical expertise to its stakeholders that helps guide their strategic investments in equipment, planning, training, and resources to enhance the resilience and protection of facilities, surrounding communities, and entire regions. We believe that the report did address these issues sufficiently. As noted in the report, IP has taken important actions to (1) standardize the selection process for RRAP project locations, (2) work with state stakeholders to better communicate the scope of projects and consider how it can share resilience information with CI partners, and (3) gather information on CI partner actions to enhance resilience after the RRAP project is completed. Nonetheless, the NIPP states that the use of performance measures is a critical step in the risk management process to enable DHS to objectively and quantitatively assess improvements in CI protection and provides a basis for DHS to document actual performance, promote effective management, and provide a feedback mechanism to decision makers. As discussed in the report, developing performance measures among and across RRAP projects could be challenging moving forward, but, absent these measures, neither we nor DHS is positioned to report on the overall success and effectiveness of the program. Hence, we recommended the development of such a mechanism to assess RRAP-related enhancements.

---

[29]In accordance with 31 U.S.C. § 720, the head of a federal agency shall submit a written statement of the actions taken on our recommendations to the Senate Committee on Homeland Security and Governmental Affairs and to the House Committee on Oversight and Government Reform not later than 60 calendar days from the date of the report and to the House and Senate Committees on Appropriations in the agency's first request for appropriations submitted more than 60 calendar days after the date of the report.

Second, DHS stated that the draft report did not substantially discuss the significant evolution of the program from a 2009 pilot to a more mature program that is at the forefront of the evolving critical infrastructure security and resilience mission that is responsive to the needs of the federal government and its partners. We disagree and believe that the report sufficiently discusses the evolution of the program, particularly the evolution of DHS's process for selecting project locations as well as changes DHS has made to address the concerns of stakeholders based on their early experiences with RRAP.

We are sending copies of this report to the Secretary of Homeland Security, the Under Secretary for the National Protection Programs Directorate, and interested congressional committees. In addition, this report is available at no charge on the GAO website at http://www.gao.gov.

If you or your staff have questions about this report, please contact me at (202) 512-8777 or caldwells@gao.gov. Contact points for our Offices of Congressional Relations and Public Affairs may be found on the last page of this report. Key contributors to this report are listed in appendix IV.

Sincerely yours,

Stephen L. Caldwell
Director
Homeland Security and Justice Issues

Appendix I: Critical Infrastructure Sectors

This appendix provides information on the 16 critical infrastructure (CI) sectors and the federal agencies responsible for sector security. The *National Infrastructure Protection Plan* (NIPP) outlines the roles and responsibilities of the Department of Homeland Security (DHS) and its partners—including other federal agencies. Within the NIPP framework, DHS is responsible for leading and coordinating the overall national effort to enhance protection via 16 critical infrastructure sectors. The NIPP and Presidential Decision Directive/PPD-21 assign responsibility for critical infrastructure sectors to sector-specific agencies (SSA).[1] As an SSA, DHS has direct responsibility for leading, integrating, and coordinating efforts of sector partners to protect 10 of the 16 critical infrastructure sectors. The remaining six sectors are coordinated by seven other federal agencies. Table 2 lists the SSAs and their sectors.

---

[1] Issued on February 12, 2013, Presidential Policy Directive/PPD-21, *Critical Infrastructure Security and Resilience*, purports to refine and clarify critical infrastructure-related functions, roles, and responsibilities across the federal government, and enhance overall coordination and collaboration, among other things. Pursuant to Homeland Security Presidential Directive/HSPD-7 and the *National Infrastructure Protection Plan*, DHS had established 18 critical infrastructure sectors. PPD-21 subsequently revoked HSPD-7, and incorporated two of the sectors into existing sectors, thereby reducing the number of critical infrastructure sectors from 18 to 16. Plans developed pursuant to HSPD-7, however, remain in effect until specifically revoked or superseded.

Table 2: Critical Infrastructure Sectors and Sector-Specific Agencies (SSA)

Critical infrastructure sector	SSA(s)[a]
Food and agriculture	Department of Agriculture[b] and the Department of Health and Human Services[c]
Defense industrial base[d]	Department of Defense
Energy[e]	Department of Energy
Government facilities	Department of Homeland Security and the General Services Administration
Health care and public health	Department of Health and Human Services
Financial services	Department of the Treasury
Transportation systems	Department of Homeland Security and the Department of Transportation[f]
Water and wastewater systems[g]	Environmental Protection Agency
Commercial facilities Critical manufacturing Emergency services Nuclear reactors, materials, and waste Dams Chemical	Department of Homeland Security • Office of Infrastructure Protection[h]
Information technology Communications	• Office of Cyber Security and Communications[i]

Source: Presidential Policy Directive/PPD-21

[a]Presidential Policy Directive/PPD-21 identifies 16 critical infrastructure sectors and designates associated federal SSAs. In some cases co-SSAs are designated where those departments share the roles and responsibilities of the SSA.

[b]The Department of Agriculture is responsible for agriculture and food (meat, poultry, and egg products).

[c]The Food and Drug Administration is the Department of Health and Human Services component responsible for food other than meat, poultry, and egg products and serves as the co-SSA.

[d]Nothing in the NIPP impairs or otherwise affects the authority of the Secretary of Defense over the Department of Defense, including the chain of command for military forces from the President as Commander in Chief, to the Secretary of Defense, to the commanders of military forces, or military command and control procedures.

[e]The energy sector includes the production, refining, storage, and distribution of oil, gas, and electric power, except for commercial nuclear power facilities.

[f]Presidential Policy Directive/PPD- 21, released in February 2013, establishes the Department of Transportation as co-SSA with the Department of Homeland Security (DHS) for the transportation systems sector. Within DHS, the U.S. Coast Guard and the Transportation Security Administration are the responsible components.

[g]The water sector includes drinking water.

[h]The Office of Infrastructure Protection is the DHS component responsible for the commercial facilities; critical manufacturing; emergency services; nuclear reactors, materials, and waste; dams; and chemical sectors.

[i]The Office of Cyber Security and Communications is the DHS component responsible for the information technology and communications sectors.

Appendix II: Criteria for Fiscal Years 2013 and 2014 RRAP Projects

This appendix provides the criteria DHS's Office of Infrastructure Protection (IP) uses to assess RRAP proposals for consideration for selection as RRAP projects. IP officials stated that the criteria were developed based on feedback received from infrastructure protection partners such as the State, Local, Tribal and Territorial Government Coordinating Council and from lessons learned conducting RRAP projects. IP officials said that they asked protective security advisors (PSA) and PSA regional directors who had previously conducted Regional Resilience Assessment Program (RRAP) projects to review the criteria before they were finalized to provide assurance that the criteria reflected lessons learned. As shown in table 3, our review of IP's criteria shows that they generally focus on the feasibility of the overall proposed project; partnering, such as whether the project has clear sponsorship and willing participants; broad applicability, such as the potential to generate resilience-related findings that can be applied to other locations; and risk-based factors, including the concentration of critical infrastructure in the region and the likelihood that the project will produce resilience-related findings.

Table 3: DHS Fiscal Years 2013 and 2014 Criteria for Identifying Candidate Regional Resiliency Assessment Projects (RRAP)

Factors of consideration	DHS guidance
Does the proposed project clearly relate to regional infrastructure resilience and the Office of Infrastructure Protection's mission?	The project should reflect the RRAP's emphasis on resilience rather than strictly security. The subject matter should be clearly within the Office of Infrastructure Protection's mission area.
Is the project concept sound?	The overall idea should seem thoughtful and logical to a potential participant. The concept should have been developed in consultation with industry or subject matter experts.
Does the proposed project have a clearly identified primary stakeholder that is willing and able to participate (e.g,. such as a state)?	This is required for success.
Does the proposed project have clearly identified and willing participants such as critical infrastructure owners and operators?	This is required for success.
Does the proposed project have the potential to contribute to a larger resilience picture or applicability beyond the focus area?	Ideally, project findings are transferable in principle to other regions or connected to part of a larger picture.
Is the proposed project likely to produce original key findings and resilience enhancement options?	The proposed project should not duplicate previous efforts in the region and subject area. The Office of Infrastructure Protection should be able to provide the stakeholder with new findings or options. At a minimum, the project should take a new angle on a known issue, or complement existing work.
Is there a plausible and compelling disruption, vulnerability, and consequence story—the negative impact of an incident on the region—associated with the proposed project's focus?[a]	Without a "yes" to all three, the project cannot proceed.
Are resilience enhancement options likely to be implemented?	Is the focus of the proposed project on the areas of highest priority for the state/region? The focus of the proposed project should be on the areas of highest priority for the state/region to increase the likelihood that resilience enhancement options will be implemented and/or reflect State, Local, Tribal and Territorial Government Coordinating Council (SLTTGCC) priorities.
Does the proposed geographic area meet the threshold (to be established each year) of concentration of critical infrastructure?	This indicates active partnerships in the operating area.

Source: DHS Office of Infrastructure Protection.

[a]According to the *National Infrastructure Protection Plan*, disruptions refer to the cascading effects resulting from an incident, such as an attack or natural disaster, on critical infrastructure assets, systems, or networks.

Appendix III: Comments from the Department of Homeland Security

U.S. Department of Homeland Security
Washington, DC 20528

Homeland Security

July 23, 2013

Stephen L. Caldwell
Director, Homeland Security and Justice Issues
U.S. Government Accountability Office
441 G Street, NW
Washington, DC 20548

Re: Draft Report GAO-13-616, "CRITICAL INFRASTRUCTURE PROTECTION: DHS Could Strengthen the Management of the Regional Resiliency Assessment Program"

Dear Mr. Caldwell:

Thank you for the opportunity to review and comment on this draft report. The U.S. Department of Homeland Security (DHS) appreciates the U.S. Government Accountability Office's (GAO's) work in planning and conducting its review and issuing this report.

DHS is pleased to note GAO's positive recognition that the Department "has taken actions to develop or update programs to assess vulnerability and risk at critical infrastructure facilities and within groups of related infrastructure regions and systems to place greater emphasis on resilience." The Regional Resiliency Assessment Program (RRAP) is one of DHS's flagship programs for infrastructure security and resilience and exemplifies the Department's focus on resilience; dedication to supporting and working collaboratively with our state, local, tribal, territorial, and private-sector partners; and the "One DHS" principle of cross-Component collaboration.

The ultimate value of the RRAP is its success in engaging our federal, state, local, tribal, territorial, and private-sector partners to collaborate on a common regional goal and in leading states and communities to adopt and implement changes to make our Nation's critical infrastructure more secure and resilient. DHS is disappointed, however, that GAO did not review and report more extensively on the overall success and effectiveness of the RRAP in assisting these partners to identify and address regional security and resilience gaps. Likewise, the draft report did not substantively discuss the significant evolution of the program from a 2009 pilot concept to what is now a more mature program that is on the forefront of the evolving critical infrastructure security and resilience mission area and which is responsive to the needs of the Federal Government and its partners.

Since the RRAP's inception, projects have been conducted in regions throughout the Nation and have focused on sectors such as Energy, Transportation, Commercial Facilities, Water, and Food and Agriculture. Through the RRAP, DHS has provided unique technical expertise to our stakeholders that helps guide their strategic investments in equipment, planning, training, and resources to enhance the resilience and protection of facilities, surrounding communities, and entire regions.

The draft report contained two recommendations with which the Department concurs. Specifically, GAO recommended that the DHS Assistant Secretary for Infrastructure Protection:

Recommendation 1: Document decisions made with regard to recommendations about individual RRAP projects to provide insights into why one project was recommended over another and assurance that recommendations among equally feasible proposals are defensible.

Response: Concur. The DHS Office of Infrastructure Protection (IP) will develop a mechanism for the next RRAP cycle, due to be conducted in Fiscal Year 2015, to more comprehensively document the decision-making process and justifications that lead to the selection of each project. Estimated Completion Date (ECD): September 30, 2014.

Recommendation 2: Develop a mechanism to assess the extent to which individual projects influenced participants to make RRAP related enhancements, such as revising the security survey and vulnerability assessment follow-up tool to query facilities that participated in RRAP projects on the extent to which any resilience improvements made are due to participation in the RRAP.

Response: Concur. DHS agrees that it would be insightful to understand whether the implementation rate of security and resilience enhancements at facilities differs between those receiving an assessment as part of the RRAP, and those receiving an assessment unrelated to this program. However, there are limitations to GAO's approach. For example, focusing on the survey tool misses facilities that participated in the RRAP but did not receive a survey or assessment. Facilities participate in the RRAP in many ways; surveys and assessments are but one option offered to facilities in the RRAP focus area. IP will review alternatives, including that offered by GAO, to collect and compare data on facilities that participated in the RRAP vice another IP engagement (other assessments, exercises, training). IP will provide additional details on how it will address this recommendation in the Department's "60 Day" letter after receipt of GAO's final report. ECD: To Be Determined.

Again, thank you for the opportunity to review and comment on this draft report. Technical comments were previously provided under separate cover. Please feel free to contact me if you have any questions. We look forward to working with you in the future.

Sincerely,

Jim H. Crumpacker
Director
Departmental GAO-OIG Liaison Office

2

Appendix IV: GAO Contact and Staff Acknowledgment

GAO Contact	Stephen L. Caldwell, (202) 512-8777 or caldwells@gao.gov
Staff Acknowledgments	In addition to the contact named above, John F. Mortin, Assistant Director, and Anthony J. DeFrank, Analyst-in-Charge, managed this assignment. Chuck Bausell, Orlando Copeland, Katherine M. Davis, Justin Dunleavy, Aryn Ehlow, Michele C. Fejfar, Eric Hauswirth, and Thomas F. Lombardi made significant contributions to the work.

Related GAO Products

*Critical Infrastructure Protection□□□ □ist of Priorit□□ssets Nee□s to □e □ali□ate□ an□ □e□orte□ to □on□ress□*GAO-13-296. Washington, D.C.: March 25, 2013.

*Critical Infrastructure Protection□Preli□inar□□□ser□ations on □□□ □fforts to □ssess □□e□ical □ecurit□□is□ an□ □at□er □ee□□ac□on □acilit□ □utreac□□*GAO-13-412T. Washington, D.C.: March 14, 2013.

*Critical Infrastructure Protection□□n I□□le□entation □trate□□□oul□ □□□ance □□□s □oor□ination of □esilience □fforts across Ports an□□□t□er Infrastructure□*GAO-13-11. Washington, D.C.: October 25, 2012.

*Critical Infrastructure Protection□□u□□ar□ of □□□ □ctions to □etter □ana□e Its □□e□ical □ecurit□Pro□ra□□*GAO-12-1044T. Washington, D.C.: September 20, 2012.

*Critical Infrastructure Protection□□□□ Is □a□in□□ction to □etter □ana□e Its □□e□ical □ecurit□Pro□ra□ □□ut It Is □oo □arl□to □ssess □esults□*GAO-12-567T. Washington, D.C.: September 11, 2012.

*Critical Infrastructure□□□□ Nee□s to □efocus Its □fforts to □ea□t□e □o□ern□ent □acilities □ector□*GAO-12-852. Washington, D.C.: August 13, 2012.

*Critical Infrastructure Protection□□□□ Is □a□in□□ction to □etter □ana□e Its □□e□ical □ecurit□Pro□ra□ □□ut It Is □oo □arl□to □ssess □esults□*GAO-12-515T. Washington, D.C.: July 26, 2012.

*Critical Infrastructure Protection□□□□ □oul□ □etter □ana□e □ecurit□ □ur□e□san□ □ulnera□ilit□□ssess□ents□*GAO-12-378. Washington, D.C.: May 31, 2012.

*Critical Infrastructure Protection□□□□ □as □a□en □ction □esi□ne□ to I□entif□an□ □□□ress □□erla□s an□ □a□s in □ritical Infrastructure □ecurit□ □cti□ities□*GAO-11-537R. Washington, D.C.: May 19, 2011.

*Critical Infrastructure Protection□□□□ □fforts to □ssess an□ Pro□ote □esilienc□□re □□ol□in□□ut Pro□ra□ □ana□e□ent □oul□ □e □tren□t□ene□□*GAO-10-772. Washington, D.C.: September 23, 2010.

*Critical Infrastructure Protection□□□□ate to National Infrastructure Protection Plan Inclu□es Increase□□□□□asis on □is□□ana□e□ent an□ □esilience□*GAO-10-296. Washington, D.C.: March 5, 2010.

*□e □e□art□ent of □o□elan□ □ecurit□s □□□□□ritical Infrastructure Protection □ost□□enefit □e□ort□*GAO-09-654R. Washington, D.C.: June 26, 2009.

*Infor□ation □ec□nolo□□□e□eral □a□s□□e□ulations□an□ □an□ator□ □tan□ar□s to □ecurin□ Pri□ate □ector Infor□ation □ec□nolo□□ □ste□s an□ □ata in □ritical Infrastructure □ectors□*GAO-08-1075R. Washington, D.C.: September 16, 2008.

*□is□ □ana□e□ent□□tren□t□enin□ t□e □se of □is□ □ana□e□ent Princi□les in □o□elan□ □ecurit□□*GAO-08-904T. Washington, D.C.: June 25, 2008.

*□ritical Infrastructure□□ector Plans □o□□lete an□ □ector □ouncils □□ol□in□□*GAO-07-1075T. Washington, D.C.: July 12, 2007.

*□ritical Infrastructure Protection□□ector Plans an□ □ector □ouncils □ontinue to □□ol□e□*GAO-07-706R. Washington, D.C.: July 10, 2007.

□ritical Infrastructure□□□allen□es □e□ain in Protectin□ □e□ □ectors□ GAO-07-626T. Washington, D.C.: March 20, 2007.

*□o□elan□ □ecurit□□Pro□ress □as □een □a□e to □□□ress t□e □ulnera□ilities □□□ose□ □□□□□□□□ut □ontinue□ □e□eral □ction Is Nee□e□ to □urt□er □iti□ate □ecurit□ □is□s□*GAO-07-375. Washington, D.C.: January 24, 2007.

*□ritical Infrastructure Protection□□Pro□ress □oor□inatin□ □o□ern□ent an□ Pri□ate □ector □fforts □aries □□ □ectors□□□aracteristics□*GAO-07-39. Washington, D.C.: October 16, 2006.

*Infor□ation □□arin□□□□□□ □□oul□ □a□e □te□s to □ncoura□e □ore □□i□es□rea□ □se of Its Pro□ra□ to Protect an□ □□are □ritical Infrastructure Infor□ation□*GAO-06-383. Washington, D.C.: April 17, 2006.

□is□ □ana□e□ent□□urt□er □efine□□ents Nee□e□ to □ssess □is□s an□ Prioriti□e Protecti□e □easures at Ports an□ □t□er □ritical Infrastructure□ GAO-06-91. Washington, D.C.: December 15, 2005.